The
Signature

Irini Zoica

Irini Zoica

Dedication

To my wonderful family, my heroin mother, the most angelic and perfect human being I have ever seen and will ever see. To my father, a man who burned himself to light us, to my brother, the greatest gift I was blessed with...and to the love of my life.

Cheers to the courage, going after our dreams…

For me, the biggest challenge was taking a pen and pouring my heart out into this book.

It starts with some hard times, dark thoughts. We are all fighting battles within ourselves. We all have dreams and goals we want to accomplish. The road there will not be easy and sometimes not even bright. We may feel alone even though we are surrounded by people.

One thing is for sure: 'I will not give up; I will walk through the dark times".

Standing alone in a small room

Looking outside the window

The world seems busy, full of life and happiness

But I sit here in silence

My mind keeps dreaming about the things I want

When are they becoming a reality?

Will I start living the way I want…

Or will I always sit alone hopelessly

My mind is full of words and desires

Waiting to be spoken and felt deeply

The day will come when I am brave enough

To make my dreams a reality!

I feel good when the night falls

The world stops.

I like it when I hear silence,

Feel good from this absence

Strange, isn't it?

Staying awake while everybody sleeps

Alone with my thoughts

Not scary at all

Just me against the world

This darkness and emptiness

Can be fulfilling

When living is so challenging

How loud my thoughts can be inside my head

Yet I'm speechless

How much my heart feels

Yet I'm silenced

What a magnificent world lives inside of me

Yet I don't express it

I am too scared to feel what I want to feel

To say what I want to say

To do what I want to do

Ah, how hard it is to clearly see

While living in the prison I put me

Takes strength to set yourself free

To finally be who you want to be

Confusion surrounds my life right now

A lot of uncertainties

Wish I knew the answer to my questions

Maybe I should take one step

And the path will show itself

Maybe I should just start

And the road will start to light

Please help!

I scream from within

I know that I can be more

But I don't know how

Please help!

I wish someone would hear my needs

And do something…

I should help myself

I am the only hope

I am the only solution

Standup! Be brave!

One step, one word

Just act

Don't be scared

Who am I?

I want to find

I don't know myself completely

If I would meet myself would I like her?

If we could talk, what would I think?

Is this what I want to be?

Who am I?

I would like to see

It's better to dream about her

And then create it to be me

They expect so much from me

I feel like I am their only hope

I wish they would start to see

That I am scared and this feels cold

They always wanted me to shine brighter

Now I don't know if I can do it

Am I able to achieve and succeed,

Or will I always cry myself to sleep

I just wish they could see my needs

Hear my voice

See my thoughts

A heavy weight to keep this is

Will I win,

Or perhaps be destroyed

Fighting and fighting and never stopping

Pushing forward without reaching the end

Finding strength from the bottom of the soul

Looking for light in the end of the road

When is it going to stop?

This exhausting journey

I cannot see the end even though I'm running

When will I stop fighting and searching for happiness?

When will I create the life, I want for myself?

The dreams I have

In my mind I can see

I'm waiting to touch them in reality

All the plans I have

For when I can be fully me

All the things

I want to achieve

I'm going step by step

Slowly,

But steadily

I'm patiently waiting

For the day

When I can fully live

It's surprising how strong I can be

Trying to find the good in everything

Always keeping a smile

Waiting for better days to come

But sometimes it's so challenging

Always waiting with optimism

Somedays I get tired

And just want to cry

Stuck between keeping a light heart

Or letting sadness capture me

I am always the one that builds others up

Emphasizing their strengths

Asking them to be brave

Pushing them in every way

Yet, I don't have the courage to believe in myself

Strange how sometimes

The days feel so long

When I just wait

For them to pass by

So many things need to be done

But I feel no motivation inside

Sometimes we take things for granted

Forgetting the value of what we have

And when those blessings leave us

We appreciate what has now left

Being stuck in my own home

Standing here all alone

The world has stopped in a way

Seems like it will never be the same

I just want to hug the people I love

To be close

And fill them with hope

I need to talk

Laugh

Go for long walks

I'm glad I have a cozy home

But it's so challenging being locked alone

- For everyone who stayed alone during the lockdown of COVID-19

I start to feel that you believe in me

And what I can achieve

But then you show me your doubts

Once again, I am fighting alone

- I know how important it is to have somebody that believes in you and supports you no matter what. Sometimes you are the only one who can see the invisible. Sometimes you will be the only one that will believe in you. Sometimes.... you have to cheer for yourself.

Surrounded by people

And still feeling lonely

Maybe I'm the one to blame,

Or maybe they don't understand

They say you get what you plant

But I am making everything I can

Making effort every day

And these dark days stay the same

I feel like everybody is doing better than me

Having better ideas,

Opportunities

I know deep inside of me

That I am good enough,

Have a lot of abilities

But this awareness is buried,

Covered with my insecurities

I have a small notebook

Where I make lists

Writing down all my goals

What I want to achieve

Strangely how in the first line

Its written:

"Get excited for living…again"

I am doing everything I can

To better myself

In every possible way

Yet I feel like I'm drowning in a deep see

Fighting to keep my head above water

And be able to breathe

- For you that are trying so hard every day, yet struggling to achieve what you want. You are not alone. This is your sign to not give up.

They always say I'm strong

I can hold myself well

They often say I don't care

I am always smiling

Appearing so confident

But sometimes when they leave,

I will start crying

Yes, I'm strong

But sometimes I'm weak

You see what I show you

But you don't know me

I don't have everything sorted out

I don't have everything under control

But they won't hear me complain

Or see me break down

I chose to fight my battles in silence

- For everyone who is fighting a secret battle within themselves, you are a strong human being and deserve respect.

The hardest thing I ever did

Going alone in a different country

People congratulated me

For them it was something big

I should feel happy and free

Yet this journey was so challenging

Walking alone in the streets

Nobody to call if there's something I need

Living a completely different lifestyle

In a strange way, it feels like my life

Turned upside down

It's not easy to fight alone

I know

Nobody you can ask for help

Nobody to give you a hand

But you have to fight this war

Even alone

You are a warrior

That wins every battle

I enjoy my own company

But sometimes it gets lonely

Being the only one in your house

Having no one to hang out

This are some dark days

I feel like they will never end

I used to enjoy every day so much

I was excited to get up

But look at me now

My life has drastically changed

I am far away from everybody I love

I used to go for long walks

Enjoy long conversations in person

Now it's only me here

Silence is the only thing I hear

I know I'm not living my life

The way I want to live

I know I'm far

From where I want to be

I'm stuck

- Some days are harder than the others. Some days feel dark, but that is okay. We need to take our time; better days will come.

I find myself full of hope sometimes

And then it changes to sad

Just like a beautiful sunny day

Being unexpectedly interrupted by rain

I wish I knew what to expect next

I find myself confused

I know what I want in my life

But the way there is dark

I wish I had the opportunity to choose

I wish I knew what I should do

This life is a very short journey

I know I should be happy

And enjoy every moment of it

I try to do this,

Believe me!

But somedays I cannot feel positive…

- It's okay not to be happy all the time. There are hard times, life has its own ups and downs. You will always go from darkness to light, just give it some time.

Irini Zoica

Sometimes, the darkest, hardest time are those that show us what really matters in life. I have learned to appreciate those few people that mean the world to me, those who give me strength.

This is for them, for the people I love and you love. For an emotion so strong that makes us wanting to keep waking, until we reach our destiny. For that emotion that is a flame that lights our way through darkness.

This is for Love...

Love

What a wholesome word

Better felt than talked

Better lived than thought

What a miracle to look into your shiny eyes

And to see the love you have for me

To hold your hand and listen to your heart beat

I want to stop the time and live this moment in eternity

Kiss your lips while the world disappears completely

Love

What a heartwarming reality

Standing both in another planet

Where exist only you and me

It's strange what impact you have in my life

I can be mad

Not wanting to talk to you

And then you come and say that you need me

I know this is true

One word is enough

One touch

One moment together

That lasts forever

I miss the days waking up

And you were there

I miss us both facing each-other

And I would stare

I miss your eyes

Your light touch

I miss me standing between your arms

The day I see you will soon come

And I will never let you go

To feel my heart again warm

And the love for you to flow

I start to write about your beauty

But I don't find a word

How to describe the face

Of somebody I love

How to describe the memories

I created with you

How to write about a thing

I only want to do

I cannot describe the music

Just listen to the sounds

I cannot define the feelings

Just like I cannot explain the colors

The way I feel when I'm with you

Is beyond compare

I become the best version of myself

You built my confidence

With your unconditional love

We grew together

Saw ourselves transform

Always stayed side by side

Experienced a love so strong

That made us build each other up

It's strange how I can be physically alone

In my small room

But feel in good company

I know I have you

Nothing can replace you being here

But at least I hear your voice

From my small computer screen

I wonder what the lovers did

Some hundred years ago

When being physically there

Was the only way to talk

I'm glad that I can hear your voice

And see your beautiful face

But you being here with me…

There's nothing I would wish instead

I am waiting for you

And cannot hold my excitement

Every second closer to you

Makes my heart beat faster

Then I see you

Standing in front of me

Everything disappears,

There are no people around us,

No buildings,

No streets

Its only you before my eyes

I burst into happy tears

I will always be your arm

When you want to cry

I will always say how bright you shine

I will always make every effort

I will always be your biggest support

You will always be my love

Never in your life

Should you feel alone

Never will I allow you

To have hopeless thoughts

And if you ever think

You are not enough

I will make you see yourself

Through my eyes

You are the first one

I want to share an exciting news with

I know that you will be as happy as me

I am sharing with you this journey

I never feel more like a woman

Than when I'm with you

There's something in the way you see me

That makes me feel so powerful

I didn't always love my body

Or appreciate what I have

I wasn't always full of confidence

But you came into my life

And made me feel perfect

You saw in me

What I never thought existed

I see myself differently now

You taught me to see myself

Through your eyes

- The power of love

Wonderful the nights I spent awake

With you

Talking in the dark

Traveling in time

Many hours would go by

But for us,

There was no such thing as time

I remember the days

I thought I wasn't doing enough

I felt weak

Without knowing why

But you were there

Always by my side

You said you adored me

That I was more than enough

For the first time in my life

I felt complete

I didn't feel the need to compete

For you, I was the best I could ever be

That was the time I started to fully live

I feel the luckiest girl alive

That a found somebody who is

My best friend

My lover

My family

All at the same time

Mother

My gracious creature, hurt mother

You only give love and need to be loved

You give everything, wanting nothing in return.

You deserve so much, you deserve the world

If I could, I would give you my heart

You gave me life, what can I give in return?

You are my heart, my soul

You inspire my world

Mother

I know this life has not been fair to you

Yet you stay right there brave and true

Your happiness and smile are the only value

You are the only real hero,

That also needs to be rescued

My father,

The wisest man I know

The one who would burn himself

To make us warm

A life with sacrifices,

Yet, a man of greatness

The one for whom his family

Is the only happiness.

I have people in my life

For whom I have unconditional love

And they turn it back to me

I learned that there is nothing

More important than family

Those few people I'm lucky to have

Who truly want to see my success

Those for whom my happiness is also theirs

Those who are my first thought when I wake up

Those who I never want to say goodbye

- We sometimes get too distracted giving our full attention to less important things, forgetting those who really matter, the ones we are lucky to have.

My father had an exhausting job

I would hear him sometimes at 2 AM,

Going to work

He would come in my room and give me a kiss

I remember every time

Even though I was half asleep

He would say goodbye to my mom at the door

And leave in the middle of the cold

I remember him coming back home

With the most tired eyes

And a back pain

Yet he never said

How overworked he felt

He would open the door with a big smile

And give us all a heartwarming hug

My mom said to me

That she felt a little sad

She was getting old every day

Her hair was turning grey

But when I look at her

I only see an ageless woman

More Goddess than human

I see my mother

And her face gives me strength

I hear her voice

And it affects me in depth

I see her smile

And the whole world changes

I touch her hand

And I wish she was ageless

My mother is my hero

My queen

My everything

A mother is just…

A mother

The most powerful word that exists

I grew up in a beautiful family

Laughing hard all day

Felt good being with them

Everyday

Now I'm far away from them

Thousands of miles keep us apart

I miss hugging them

Being there to help

I know they need me

I need them too

It's hard as it is

The words cannot tell

How much I miss you

- For all the people that live far away from their loved ones, far away from their family, parents.

There is one person

I aspire being similar to

My mother

The woman with a golden heart

The one who stayed the same

Patient and tolerant

Gracious and polite

Always wise

We are all different and unique

But I would be the luckiest girl alive

If I would ever be half as kind

No matter how far I go

There is a place I call home

A place that helped me grow

A place where I belong

I will always go back

Even if I'm gone for too long

I wish I could see my mother

When she was young

What happened to her

That made her so strong

What people did she meet,

That taught her to love

How many times she got laughed at

And yet became so confident

I have learned from her so much,

I will never stop

But the things she can teach me

Are never enough

Irini Zoica

It takes a lot of strength to believe in yourself. It's the only way to go ahead. Wonderful are all those people who appreciate others around them, but the greatest people are those who also appreciate themselves.

I admire all the powerful women that with their success proved to me that I can fulfill every dream I have. They are the living proof that you own your life. I admire all the wise women who know their worth, know who they are, who love themselves.

There is no way you can stay in the darkness, when you have light within you.

Love yourself, if you do this, you have already won.

Beautiful flower my mother said

Your body is

Blooming seed she referred to it

To love my body, she taught me

Maybe because for her, nobody did

I come from a family where women

Were far ahead of their time

Women who were mothers, sisters, daughters, wives

Women who never cared if they were judged

Those with vision who would never stop

Those who would go against everyone

And show the whole world who they really are

Women who loved, believed, laughed, cried

Suffered,

And wanted to be free

I come from a long line of women

Who were many times defeated

But then came back stronger

With every blessing that they needed

Who am I to let them down?

I will use my every power

To continue this old tradition

Where every woman builds a ladder

That grows tall generation after generation

Love yourself just the way you are

See your beauty and don't forget to smile

Feel your power from within

Turn into the best version of your dreams

I stay in front of a mirror

And I love what I see

That imperfect skin

I am not embarrassed

To show my bare face

I don't care about the beauty standards

The society has set

I decide if I'm pretty for myself

I've heard women say they don't feel pretty

But beauty was all I could see

They were passionate

They were smart

They were strong

They were wise

There is no woman not pretty enough

I've seen beauty inside their hearts

I have seen girls hating their bodies

Wishing they could change every part of it

But in my eyes, everything was where it should be

Who cares about how the perfect body looks

According to society

If such thing as perfection exists

Its inside you,

Its inside me

I never compare myself to other women

They are not my competition

They are my inspiration

There is no place for rivalry

They are not taking anything away from me

Those who have achieved what I want to achieve

Prove to me that I can turn my dreams into reality

I learned to be confident in my own skin

Even though it isn't clear

I have a lot of acne scars

Which some people saw with disgust

I never tried to cover them

I feel pretty in my own skin

Never felt embarrassed in any way

Learned to love myself just the way I am

She was full of passion

Her heart was made of love

Desire was burning into her soul

She was wise

Knew her goals

Would always fight, even alone

She was strong

Confident enough

Never in her life did she give up

She always had her head up

She knew who she was from the start

She said her past destroyed her

Left wounds that couldn't be seen

She said her past imprisoned her

Tied with chains of sad memories

She said her past impacted her so much

She could never recover again

But I believe everyone has a second chance

We are so strong and powerful

To get up and start again

To find the courage within us

To forgive,

But not forget

For us,

Not for them

This woman was far from perfect

She never intended to be

She knew her worth

Her values were all she could see

Yes, she was not complete

Maybe she would never be

Growing and developing was for her a need

This woman had still a lot to fix within herself

Yet she would never accept somebody's else disrespect

This is how much she loved herself

The Signature

I owe it to myself

To practice self-care

To be my biggest fan

To applaud my success

I owe it to myself

To gently talk about me

And respect what I feel

There is no one else

That can love me best

I owe it to myself

You do everything you can

But you don't receive

A good word back

You try so hard

And just need them to appreciate

But you get disrespect instead

You do your best

But your struggles are never seen

Maybe it is just so hard for them

To acknowledge your success

Maybe you are so good

They try in silence to hate

Or choose to make you feel bad

Sometimes we are our worst enemy

Hating our bodies

More than anything

Sometimes we are the only ones

Not able to see our beauties

The wonderful creature

That is nothing less than magical

I want to make sure

I never look back

And feel regret

For not appreciating myself

The power of women cooperating

Is so fascinating

What we can do together

Is extraordinary

The power of women

Is revolutionary

Such a wonderful gift

To build each other up

Such a bless

That only brings happiness

Woman,

You powerful gracious woman

The beginning of life

The light in the dark

Stay proud

Stay strong

You wise wonderful women

I didn't feel confident expressing my thoughts

It felt inappropriate to say my opinion openly

But when I started writing, this changed my world

I feel powerful when I write in lines

It's an open door through my mind

It brings me joy and contentment

Being able to express myself

Strange how when I write

I am in peace with my mind

- Find your passion. Do something that makes you feel good. It doesn't have to be related to your profession or something you will be paid for. For as long as it makes you feel happy, calm or even distracts you for some minutes, it is worth your time.

I admire those strong women

Who go after what they believe

Those who are not afraid

To fully express themselves

Those who started from zero

And arrived where they always dreamed

I admire those independent women

Who know how to live on their own

Those who are concentrated

To fully grow

Those who are the last to go to bed

And the first to wake up again

You are worth being admired

You are those who inspire

I am full of love

Love for myself

Love for who I am

But it hasn't always been this way

It took a long time

To be able to see

I said to the mirror

'I have all I need'

There were many times

I repeated this

Took a lot of strength

To finally believe it

My mother has always been an initiator

All her fears disappear

When she has a dream to achieve

She becomes more than a human

Her motivation is astonishing

I learned from her many things

But the one thing she proved to me

Is that it doesn't matter where I start,

Doesn't matter who I am

I can always make the first step

I can always initiate

I am a human only physically

There is no limit on what I can achieve

The way she talks,

Wins

Is for me breathtaking

Nothing shines brighter

Through my eyes

Than the delight I feel

When I think about the future me

I remember one day

I was in my favorite outfit

Walking so confidently

Down the street

I saw three girls staring at me

One of them said 'look at her skin'

'Look at how terrible it is'

Just because I had acne,

I was a teen

Her comment didn't affect me

But made me think

How much power we have within our words

Yet, some still choose to hurt

Beautiful gesture to make a compliment

Or not to speak

When there is nothing nice to say

If you want to be treated a certain way

Start by treating yourself the same

This way you teach others how to act

In your presence

I promise you

If someone cares enough

They will find the time

They will prioritize

Never allow someone to disrespect you

They will think you accept to be treated that way

They did it once, they can do it again

See the value you have

You deserve respect

Never settle for less

How can you not be confident

Seeing what you have been through

Yet every battle made you more powerful

Take a look back,

A few years ago

Now look at how far you have come

How magnificently you developed

You are like a butterfly

Once scared

Now not afraid to fight

Sometimes you close your eyes and see

What you are able to achieve

Who you can really be

That is your true self

Bring her to the surface

If nobody said to you today

How lucky they are to have you

Know it for yourself

That you have so much values

I know how amazing it is

To feel appreciated,

If nobody has done this with you

Doesn't mean they think it's not true

People are quick to say what they don't like

But when we see something we love,

Something nice

We choose not to say it sometimes

Let me be the one to share with you a truth

You are so much more

Than you think you know

Never change for others

To make them, like you more

But change for yourself

If this helps you develop

I saw I couldn't fit in

In many groups of friends

And this is okay

Made me find other people

With whom I was myself

I love to see myself

Dressed up, with makeup on

But I feel the same way

When I'm in my baggy clothes

And don't put any effort at all

If there is someone

I own an apology

Its myself

For all the times I doubted me

For all the times I didn't believe

For holding myself back

For making me feel bad

For every time I didn't appreciate

Who I am

Magnificent those women

Who dare to try,

Those who are not afraid to fail

And never give up

They make mistakes along the way

There's no such thing as 'always success'

They fall

But stay strong

Then rise up again

Higher than before

And then, I saw the light…

Hope

Getting excited about living again

These last months have been hard,

Empty,

Lonely

I was asking myself when I would see the light

When I would feel alive

Now I'm waking up with a new hope

That I can finally see happiness,

Success

The world seems colorful when you can see

Yourself approaching towards your destiny

When the day starts dark

And the night is bright

Will I stop trying

Or worse, give up!

What a wonderful feeling waking up

And seeing the sun shining through the window

Listening to children playing outside

Everything starting to bloom again

What a dark winter this has been

What a hard time just existing

But the spring now gives me hope

And I cannot stop dreaming

I am waiting for the day I don't feel alone

The day I stop being on my own

I need love

I need warmth

I need happiness that will start and grow

I need to be brave and strong

And keep trying again and again

I need to keep moving on

No matter how many close doors I face

I need to believe in myself

Even if I am the only one

Doesn't matter how many times I cry

Doesn't matter how hard it becomes

Nobody will take me out of the dark

I am the only one that can make myself shine

They told me I am not good enough

That I would never do it

Little did they know that those words

Started a fire in my soul

A fire so big that burned my insecurities

Built my strength

Made them not able to talk to me again

Made me proud

Made me win

You my dear,

Are the greatest creation of life

Look around

There is no one else like you

I know you are passionate,

Eager to live

Full of love

Wanting to be loved

Next time you judge or doubt yourself

Remember

You are the chosen one

I find myself worrying sometimes

That my journey is becoming very hard

Then I remember that there is first a caterpillar

Before turning into a butterfly

- *The best things in life never come easily. Most of the time we have to earn them. In the end, everything will turn out fine. Just trust the process.*

Isn't it sad that people envy

When you win

They wish to see you down

And fail

Some cheer for you

For as long as you don't do better than them

Some others smile in your face

And then hate behind your back

If you want everybody to love you

You should do nothing

Say nothing

Be nothing

No,

I prefer to be judged and disliked

While I express my voice

And live in my own way

Rather than being praised and liked

By paying the silence and weakness price

I love the power of words

Seeing people smile after a compliment

Changing their whole day in a second

It's like having a magical wand

This gift is so forceful

Yet many use it to tear others apart

I use them to save and give people strength

I choose to spread love

To show them respect

And from their eyes,

I get so much more back

You are so beautiful

Never forget to tell yourself

It's not a lie

It's an acknowledgment

Look at your eyes

How much they have seen

Look at your lips

Passionately they have kissed

Look at your body

What it has been through

You are not only beautiful,

You are a muse

- You are beautiful. Learn to love yourself before anybody else. You deserve love – be the first one to love yourself.

I know that a whole world lies inside of you

To the shy girl that chooses to never speak

I know your words are dry

But your thoughts could fill an ocean

I know you choose to be quiet

But you are very loud from the inside

- I have been one of you. Never judge someone before knowing them well first. Some people are much more than they choose to show.

How lucky we are to be so unique

There's only one me that exists

There's only one me that has ever lived

We have the power to be and create

Something so different, so diverse

Forget what is doing somebody else

Always embrace your uniqueness

If they don't show respect

Show them how they need to act

By loving yourself

Show them how you should be treated

How much you deserve

Always know your values

Know your worth

From all the feelings and emotions, we have

Many people choose to hate

They have anger within themselves

What a miserable way to live

Poisoning yourself with jealousy

Wishing others ill

Unfortunate to forget that hate

Only hurts them back

I am scared

But fear is not a negative thing

It's an emotion that shows me

That I am in the right direction

Pushes me to keep walking

Doesn't let me give up

If we would play it safe all the time

We would just stop

We wouldn't grow up

It's so easy to do something you can already do

Dare to be scared

Get out of your comfort zone

It's the only way!

I know a girl

That has been through a lot

She failed at times

But succeeded above all

Life is full of ups and downs

The failures became for her a lesson

Made her wiser,

She learned to resist,

After every breakdown

She created a masterpiece

Impossible

I love this word

I cannot count all the times

I heard 'it's impossible'

How many times they said this to me

And I just stayed quiet

The moment I turned their impossible

Into my reality

Was enough to shut them down

And make myself proud

As the time passed

I started to know myself better

I discovered new things about me

That I never thought existed

Maybe they weren't there before

Maybe they are created after every experience,

Achievement,

Hard time,

All I know is that I love who I am

And I am eager to discover who I will be in the future

I see a strong, confident woman

The woman I dreamed of being

That insecure little girl

Witnessed a wonderful transformation

That keeps growing

Keeps going

Sure, I have a lot of wishes

But I am happy with what I have

If only everybody would know

How rich they really are

I am glad to have eyes

And watch the sun rise

I am happy to have a house

And be warm in rainy days

I am lucky to have people

Who love me as much as I love them

I have more than enough

I am blessed in every way

If you ever doubt yourself

Know that you are enough

There are people that you inspire

Even though you may not know

There are people that look at you

And admire

They stay and stare

Even though you may not be aware

Be proud of yourself

You make them want to be more

So be confident,

You are what they are looking for

To achieve what I want in life

To succeed

There's nothing holding me back

To develop myself

To create what I deserve

To inspire people

There is no other way

There is no need for immediate,

Big change

But doing small things everyday

In a great way

I know I have the power within me

From the desire I feel

It burns deep inside my heart

It lives in my mind

I know I have the power within me

I have desire

That's all I need

Never get disappointed

Over something you didn't achieve

Something better is coming

This, I always believe

I've been so afraid

To speak up my mind

To say what I think

In fear of being judged

Only now I understand

That words are my right

It took a long time

To be confident enough

There are many things I need to do

Even when I just want to stay in bed

Pushing myself to get up and move

It's the only way I can help myself

Sometimes I feel discouraged

See no point of trying so hard

Then the vision of the life I have in mind

Makes me go on and never stop

She said she wanted to do it

But she didn't even try

Maybe she was afraid,

Or she didn't want it enough

Every time I achieved success

They tried to fade my happiness

By trying to show they achieved bigger things

That they were doing better than me

Even though there was no need to compete

We are all accomplished, competent

We do great in different ways

Why shutter somebody's confidence

When we can build them up instead,

Support,

Congratulate

I feel a fire grow inside of me

A crazy desire to be free

To finally believe in me

To live my life the way I dream

Working hard towards your goals

Is truly a challenge

A journey full of difficulties,

Sometimes failures,

The end is hard to see

But there is no better feeling

Than achieving success

After a long exhausting storm

Your efforts start to take form

I was the one who would awkwardly smile

When my friends laughed out loud

I would walk alone behind the group

Feeling almost invisible to them

Like I was in the wrong place

Made me lose my confidence

But along the way I found myself

They were similar drops forming the rain

I was like a rainbow coming after them

Being different is okay

It's easy to forget the present

By constantly thinking about the future

Worrying about what will happen next

Trying to plan everything ahead

But for this exact moment here

We used to worry in the past

The past no longer exists

The future is not yet here

But this present moment right now

This is real

People will not always believe in your dreams

They can't take your eyes and see

Show them the results

When the dream becomes reality

People will always judge

You can never please everyone

You shouldn't even try

This is YOUR life

- People will judge because they don't know you well, or maybe they know you and want to make you feel bad. Strange reasons they may have, some of them we may not understand. If it makes your heart happy, and doesn't damage anyone, go ahead and do it, follow your dreams. There is no one you should please, besides yourself.

The biggest goal of my life

Is to be able to inspire

Doesn't matter if I inspire thousands

Or millions of people

It could be only one

And that would be my biggest achievement

For everything I do in life

I have two questions in mind

Does it bring me happiness?

Will I be able to affect, help?

And if the answer is 'yes'

There is for me no greater success

You know those days when you just want to lay in bed

But you feel guilty for not finishing any tasks

Sometimes our body needs a break

And our mind needs to rest

Its okay to have one of those days

Allow them,

Don't feel guilty instead

Take good care of yourself

They said I've changed,

That I was not the same anymore

Like this was a bad thing

Who would want to stay the same,

Without the possibility to change?

I want to see myself develop,

Grow in every way

When they say 'You have changed'

I answer 'Good, that's what I intend'

Such a miraculous feeling

To wake up and feel alive

After all those dark times

I was so afraid to initiate,

Create

To walk into the unknown

When there was no direction shown

It was a very long wait

And the directions never came

It gave me courage to take the first step

And the path showed itself

They said I couldn't,

That I never would

Over and over again

But in my heart

Was only one truth

I created a vision for myself

A plan that would help me go ahead

I was the only one who believed

I said I will

And I did

I can see the light in the darkness

Hear the silence

Dream when the night is gone

Feel complete even when I'm alone

-I am enough

I waited so much

For the right time to come

Until I got tired

I decided that this moment is now

I will create it

I just started from scratch

A caste is built

Stone after stone

- The time is now

The most meaningful thing I can achieve

Is to inspire someone

Even unintentionally,

Somebody I know

Or somebody I will never meet

I know I said I didn't want anything from anyone

I said I would do it all by myself

I wasn't being selfish

I want to achieve the things I want

On my own

Even if I will do it the hard way

I appreciate your desire to help

But there is no greater support

Than cheering for me

And believing in my dream

That's all I need

I learned to work towards my goals silently

So other people wouldn't ruin it

Finding thousands of reasons why I couldn't do it

I learned to keep everything to myself

Quietly achieve my success

There were very few people I would share my happiness

And for others…

They see the results when my goal is complete

Extraordinary what moment of proudness I feel

Don't be afraid to be challenged

Even if you face some failures

It will make you develop

Learn the lessons

You will come back a greater person

Sometimes we are so eager to reach the destination,

We fail to enjoy the amazing journey

Rebirth

I see the trees

Losing their leaves in winter

And blooming again in spring

'I will rise too'

I say to myself

We are part of the nature

Extraordinary creatures

After every storm and rain

The sun shines again

They have made me feel bad

I never do the same

It takes too much energy

And I have my vision clear

I just remember

And then do better

For myself

I spend all my energy to create,

Achieve success in every step

This is the best revenge

There are many battles I have won in silence

I celebrate with myself

There are some moments of happiness

I choose not to share

When there is darkness

And you see no light

That is the moment

You should fight twice as hard

The best feeling in the world

Was falling in love

With myself

Becoming who I always wanted to be

Waking up more confident every day

Getting more passionate

Creating bigger dreams

Feeling fulfilled

It requires strength

To finally be proud of yourself

And your biggest fan

Getting ready to live

The life I deserve

I caught myself saying

'I don't want to do this anymore'

But I'm the one who allowed it

And only I can make it stop

Believing in what I couldn't see

Made me touch what I once dreamed

We are the ones that create our life

If there is something we don't like

We are the only ones

That can make it stop

I know that it would be wonderful

To have somebody

That will save you from all the struggles

Show you the right way,

How you should act,

What to do next

But most of the times,

It doesn't work this way

You are the only one

That has to fight for yourself

I know it's not easy

Sometimes it's not even fair

But thinking about it…

It's the best way

I repeat to myself

"I can achieve everything I want"

Not because I don't believe it

But because I want this phrase

Stuck in my mind,

My heart

So that it will destroy every fear,

Or doubt

I always try to compliment someone

If there is something about them, I like

It's just a simple sentence from me

But I can see their smiles,

Cheerful eyes

On each-other, so much impact we have

Enough that some positive words

Can change somebody's day

Always seek success,

Having goals,

Big plans

Dare to dream big

It allows you to be free

The Signature

If you made it to the end...I want to say THANK YOU!

This was a journey. I wish you feel inspired, you appreciate and value yourself.

Wanting to do better every day is a great thing, but first, be comfortable with the person you are.

I feel like you are my friend now, even though I may never meet you.

If you were expecting for a sign to go after your dreams, to do what would make you happy, this is it.

Go ahead!

Don't forget to love yourself!

Made in the USA
Las Vegas, NV
12 February 2022

43781526R00089